THE LITTLE BOOK OF

SKIING

First published in 2022 by OH! An imprint of Welbeck Publishing Group Limited.

The right of Malcolm Croft to be identified as the Author of the Work has been asserted by him in accordance with the Copyright, Designs and Patents Act 1988.

This edition published by OH
An Imprint of Headline Publishing Group Limited

Cataloguing in Publication Data is available from the British Library

ISBN 978-1-80069-201-5

Compiled and written by: Malcolm Croft
Editorial: Victoria Denne
Designed and typeset in Joanna Nova by: Tony Seddon
Project manager: Russell Porter
Production: Arlene Lestrade
Printed and bound in China

Headline's policy is to use papers that are natural, renewable and recyclable products and made from wood grown in well-managed forests and other controlled sources. The logging and manufacturing processes are expected to conform to the environmental regulations of the country of origin.

HEADLINE PUBLISHING GROUP
An Hachette UK Company
Carmelite House, 50 Victoria Embankment, London EC4Y 0DZ
www.headline.co.uk   www.hachette.co.uk

THE LITTLE BOOK OF
SKIING

A CELEBRATION OF DOWNHILL, OFF-PISTE AND APRÈS-SKI

CONTENTS

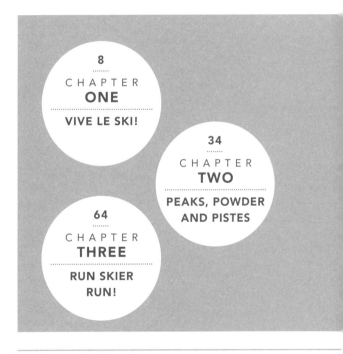

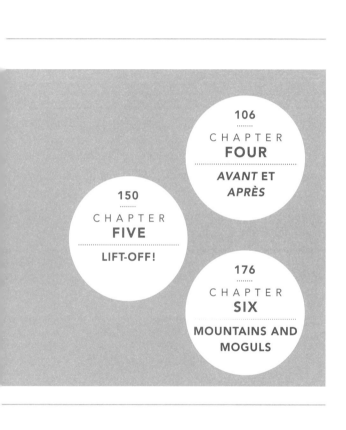

INTRODUCTION

Kick off those boots. Hang up those poles. Slip off those wet salopettes, slide into an Aperol Spritz (or three) and join us at the bar for some well-deserved après-ski. Yes, it's time to raise your *schnapps*, give thanks to the Norse god and goddess of skiing, Ullr and Skade, and toast to a day spent *schussing* down slopes of all shapes and sizes (hopefully) in some sort of style. Because, as champion hotdogger Glen Plake once famously said, "Skiing is the best way in the world to waste time," and he could not have been more spot-on.

Skiing is indeed the greatest thing in the world you can do standing up. It's also the most fun way in the world to fall down. If only it wasn't so bloody difficult to get up again, skiing would be practically perfect in every way. Think about it…

That *click* of a ski binding into place; that *whir* of the lift as it pushes you to the peak; that *crunch* of a fresh dump (not that); that *whoosh* of fresh wind as you plunge off the edge; that *swish* of a swift stem christie; that euphoric smug *snort* of pulling those achy-breaky boots off… Yes, skiing contains a multitude of sights, sounds, smells and sensations that soak your senses in super-fun-time endorphins and chemicals. For the 400 *million* global plankers, slope dopes, run bums, and mogul-maniacs, skiing is truly the only way to get an all-natural high, without a hangover. (That comes *après*.)

So, to honour humankind's multi-millennia obsession with this snowy sport and popular well-powdered pastime – and the 160th anniversary of the first ever ski-jump competition in 1862, FYI – *The Little Book of Skiing* is here to celebrate everything ski-based in bitesize book form. From steezy ski lingo to shredded stats, ice-cold facts to super-cool quotes, and everything awesome in between, this tiny tome is your ideal slope-side companion and après ski drinking buddy. It's an ode so gnarly, it's waist deep in wisdom and the perfect read for powder hounds of all skill levels, from bunny riders to black diamond hunters.

So, *Skål* – here's to falling down mountains in style.

See you at the top, brah…

CHAPTER
ONE

Vive le Ski!

As U2 once famously sang, "Get on your boots!" Yep, it's time to take to the mountain and show the snow who's boss. For skiers, making first tracks in fresh powder is the best way to start the day. So, what are we waiting for? It's snow time…

Spores

Stupid People On Rental Equipment

The largest interconnected ski region in the world is Les Trois Vallées, France. The 372 miles (600km) of linked valleys, trails and slopes are joined by 183 ski lifts, all available through a single ski pass. The lifts transport 260,000 skiers per hour there are more than 3,000 ski instructors on-site every season.

The region contains the best ski resorts in the world: Courchevel, Meribel, La Tania, Brides-les-Bains, Val Thorens, Les Menuirens, Saint-Martin Belleville and Orelle.

The world's longest
ski run is the 13-mile
(20km) Valle Blanche in
Chamonix, France.

Bob Smith, Dentist

It was a Californian ski-freak named Bob Smith, a dentist by day, whom we have to thank for inventing the revolutionary fog-resistant ski goggle. "In skiing powder, snow would get inside the goggle through the vent holes, and the humidity would go way up, and, with a single lens … the thing got foggy," Smith told *Powder* magazine in 1981.

In 1965, Smith innovated the dual-pane lens with breathable foam vents that prevented fogging, freezing and condensation. It's yet to be bettered.

Après Ski Drinks #1: France

According to sno.co.uk, these are the top après-ski drinks in France:

Vin chaud: A warm red wine with spices and orange.

Demi-peche: A shot of peach syrup in French beer; a posh shandy.

Chocolat chaud: Hot chocolate. Add whisky for adults.

Génépi: Herbal liqueur (as a palate cleanser).

Toffee vodka: No introduction necessary.

Ski UK

According to Red Bull, these are the UK's most popular ski destinations:

1. Glenshee Ski Centre – the largest ski area in Scotland with over 40km of pistes!

2. Lecht 2090, Aberdeenshire

3. Glencoe Mountain Resort, Rannach Moor

4. Nevis Mountain Range Resort, Fort William

5. Cairngorm Ski Resort, Aviemore

6. Midlothian Snowsports Centre, Edinburgh – biggest outdoor dryslope in the UK!

7. Raise, Cumbria

8. Yad Moss, Cumbria/ Durham

9. Allenheads, Northumberland

10. Storey Arms, Brecon

Winter Olympic Medal Table: Alpine Skiing 1936–2022

	Gold	Silver	Bronze	Total
1. Austria	7	4	8	19
2. France	5	4	2	11
3. Switzerland	4	5	5	14
4. United States	2	0	1	3
5. Norway	1	5	1	7
6. Italy	1	1	1	3
7. Germany	0	1	1	2
8. Canada	0	0	2	2

Ski Resorts by US State: Top 15

According to Statista, these are
America's top ski areas by state:

1. New York – 51

2. Michigan – 40

3. Wisconsin – 31

4. Colorado – 31

5. New Hampshire – 30

6. California – 30

7. Pennsylvania – 26

8. Vermont – 23

9. Minnesota – 20

10. Maine – 18

11. Idaho – 17

12. Utah – 15

13. Montana – 15

14. Washington – 14

15. Massachusetts – 13

Skiing Playlist #1: Snow

"Snow (Hey oh)" – Red Hot
Chilli Peppers
"Let it Snow" – Frank Sinatra
"Fifteen Feet of Pure White Snow"
– Nick Cave and the Bad Seeds
"Cold As Ice" – Foreigner
"Velvet Snow" – Kings of Leon
"Don't Eat the Yellow Snow"
– Frank Zappa
"Snow-blind" – Black Sabbath
"Snowbound" – Genesis
"White As Snow" – U2
"The Icicle Melts" – Cranberries

Suki ni ikimashyo!

"Let's go skiing!"
in Japanese.

Skibootigasm*

That euphoric feeling of kicking heavy ski boots off tired feet, otherwise known as footsore, after a long day skiing. The discomfort is caused by tight-fitting boots, uneven pressure distribution and/or inflexibility.

*OK, we've made this one up, as a specific word doesn't seem to exist – but should!

66

You let yourself go. Gliding delightfully over the gentle slopes, flying down the steeper ones, taking an occasional cropper, but getting as near to flying as any earthbound man can. In that glorious air it is a delightful experience.

99

Sir Arthur Conan Doyle

The subtle hourglass shape of a ski, as viewed from the top, is called the sidecut.

According to the 2020
International Report
on Snow & Mountain
Tourism, 400 million
people go skiing around
the world every ski season.

Ski

The word "ski" takes its
origins from the Old
Norse word skiõ
– which once meant
"a stick of wood".

Little Ripper

The scientific term for a toddler or young child that flies down a black run with absolutely zero fear.

Typically, an adult male (the largest demography of skiers) will burn approximately 400 calories an hour downhill skiing. A day's skiing will burn approx. 1,500 calories.*

*A typical après-skier will consume more than 1,500 calories in alcohol. You do the math.

Nobody Does it Better

James Bond became a true British (and global) icon when, in *The Spy Who Loved Me* (1977), he executed perhaps the most famous ski movie scene in history, all while being chased by Soviet agents off a Swiss cliff… only to rip open a Union Jack parachute in time for Carly Simon to belt out the theme, "Nobody Does it Better".

Stuntman Rick Sylvester performed the dangerous jump in one take from the top of Asgard Peak, Baffin Island, Canada, for a fee of $30,000.

Schussing

To bomb down the
slope without turning.

Hucking

Jumping off a cornie – an overhang, cliff or steep edge. Go huck a cornie!

Cold Smoke

Supremely light and powdery snow. The kind you want to eat.

"

For me, personally, skiing holds everything. I used to race cars, but skiing is a step beyond that. It removes the machinery and puts you one step closer to the elements. And it's a complete physical expression of freedom.

"

Robert Redford

Apres Ski Drinks #2: Italy

According to sno.co.uk, these are the top après-ski drinks in Italy:

Aperol spritz: Aperol liqueur, prosecco, and soda water with orange peel.

Bombardino: ¾ hot traditional egg liquor, ¼ rum or brandy, topped with whipped cream. "The bomb", in Italian.

Caffé corretto: Italian coffee with a shot of grappa, sambuca or brandy.

No Ski Sherlock

Believe it or not, it was the British author Sir Arthur Conan Doyle, of Sherlock Holmes stories, who introduced skiing…to Switzerland.

Doyle would often enjoy ski trips in Norway. One day, on a trip to Switzerland, he took along his skis, as he felt it could be full of sick runs. "I am convinced that the time will come when hundreds of English men will come to Switzerland for the skiing season," he remarked after.

CHAPTER
TWO

Peaks, Powder and Pistes

There are so many things to love about skiing. From all the gnarly gear to the mountain vistas, the taste of fresh snow after your first fall to the fireside chats with après-skiers, skiing has a little bit of awesome for everyone. Only one question remains: Red or black?

Today, there are approximately 2.6 injuries per 1,000 skier days. The knee, particularly the rupture of the anterior cruciate ligament (ACL), is the most frequent sore point, accounting for 35 per cent of all skiing injuries.

Modern ski bindings have an automatic self-release which pops the leg free from the ski to help prevent severe knee twists and turns.

Stand Up!

Keep falling over? Of course you do – it's skiing. It's part of the fun! To stand up again, just follow these five simple steps:

1. Place your skis downhill from you, so that they're parallel, or pointing slightly uphill, to the slope. Dig the edges of your skis into the snow for grip.

2. Keep your hands free; so plant your poles into snow nearby.

3. Bend your knees and turn your upper body towards the snow. Place both hands down, and push down to lift your hips, keeping your knees bent.

4. Grab your poles. Use them to push yourself to a standing stance.

5. Dig your toes and heels into the bindings. Away you go…

Amplitude

Any gnarly height a skier achieves in the air when skiing off a halfpipe, ramp, jib or jump.

66

With luck, it might even snow for us.

99

Haruki Murakami

"

Snowflakes are one of nature's most fragile things, but just look what they can do when they stick together.

"

Vesta M. Kelly

"

Summer friends
will melt away like
summer snows, but
winter friends are
friends forever.

"

George R.R. Martin

Après Ski Drinks #3: Austria

According to sno.co.uk, these are the top après-ski drinks in Austria:

Schnapps: Apricot, pear, apple or peach liqueur, downed as a shot.

Glühwein: Warm red wine with sugar, cinnamon, cloves, and fresh orange.

Spezi: Cola with orange soda.

Stiegl: Austria's No.1 beer brand.

Jagertee: Black tea and rum punch.

Yard Sale

A wipe-out on the slopes so epic it causes the skier to litter their gear all over the slope.

Flügel

An energy drink
mixed with vodka.
#1 après-ski drink
for skiers under 25.

"

Skiing combines outdoor fun with knocking down trees with your face.

"

Dave Barry

Ski School

What level are you?

Level 1 *First Timer* – never skied before

Level 2 *Early Learner* – snowploughs on nursery slopes

Level 3 *Learner* – linking snowploughs

Level 4 *Early Improver* – snowploughs on green slopes

Level 5 *Improver* – slow parallel turns on blue and green runs

Level 6 *Early Intermediate* – slow on red runs

Level 7 *Intermediate* – reds and most black runs in good conditions

Level 8 Early Advanced – all on-piste runs

Level 9 Advanced – fast on black runs

Level 10 Early Expert – fast on all runs and off-piste

Level 11 Expert – ski fluidly on or off-piste anywhere on mountain

Level 12 Athletes & Instructor Trainers – can ski any where, any time, any way.

Level 13 God – I'm on TV during the Winter Olympics

Indie Grab

Grabbing the skis under the boot on the outside edge midway through a jump. Looks cool.

Kick Turn

Turning 180 degrees while stationary by lifting one ski and reversing its direction, followed by the other ski.

❝

Après-ski is my favourite sport.

❞

Barbara Walters

Know Thy Mondopoint

Convert your foot size into Mondopoint...

Mondopoint (CM)	UK	EU	U.S. Men	U.S. Women
24	5	3	8	6 7
24.5	5.5	38.5	6.5	7.5
25	6	39	7	8
25.5	6.5	40	7.5	8.5
26	7	40.5	8	9
26.5	7.5	41	8.5	9.5
27	8	42	9	10
27.5	8.5	42.5	9.5	10.5
28	9	43	10	11
28.5	9.5	44	10.5	11.5
29	10	44.5	11	12

*The Mondopoint System is the global standard for measuring ski boot sizes, offering a much better fit – it takes width and length into account.

Bond on the Run

James Bond's love of skiing in his novel is due to author Ian Fleming's early life living in the exclusive Austrian ski resort, Kitzbühel. These are the times Bond has skied on screen…so far!

On Her Majesty's Secret Service (1969)
Mürren (Switzerland)

The Spy Who Loved Me (1977)
St Moritz (Switzerland)

For Your Eyes Only (1981)
Cortina d'Ampezzo (Italy)

The Living Daylights (1986)
Weißensee (Austria)

The World Is Not Enough (1999)
Chamonix (France)

Spectre (2015)
Sölden (Austria)

Cornie

An overhanging edge
of snow on a ridge of a
mountain with a sharp
drop underneath.

Jerry

A skier who attempts to do a skiing manoeuvre or technique that is greatly above their skill level or ability.

Ski Three

Skiing comes in three forms.

How do you like to do it?

1. Alpine, or downhill, skiing. Fixed-heel bindings of ski to boot.

2. Nordic – cross-country skiing and ski jumping. Boots are not bound to heel.

3. Telemark – a mix of alpine and Nordic skiing; squatting on skis with boots not bound to heel.

In 2021, more than 14.6 million Germans went skiing – the highest number of any European nation. In second was France, with 8.5 million skiers, and in third place, with 6.3 million skiers was the UK.

Skiing on the Moon

Several Apollo astronauts compared walking on the Moon to skiing. Most notably was Apollo 17 astronaut, Harrison "Jack" Schmitt. "Too bad I don't have my skis!" Schmitt told Houston Command while walking on the moon. Schmitt even invented "lunar cross-country skiing" while on the surface of Earth's satellite.

"In the moon's low gravity, you can ski above the moondust – and I did. Imagine swinging your arms and legs cross-country style. With each push of your toe, your body glides forward above ground. Swing, glide, swing, glide. The only marks you leave in the moondust are the toe-pushes."

The most expensive adult day lift pass in Europe is in Sölden, a glacier ski resort in the Austrian province of Tyrol.

It costs €64 a day.

The Arlberg System

If you've been taught to
ski from basic snowplough
stop and turns, to stem and
stem christie/parallel turns,
then you were schooled
in the progressive Arlberg
System. This technique
was created by Hannes
Schneider, an instructor in
the Arlberg mountains, Austria.
It became popular in the
US the 1920s.

Allez viens, on va skier!

"Come on, let's go skiing!" in French.

In 2020, the market size of the ski and snowboard resorts industry in the United States stood at 2.53 billion US dollars.

According to Statista, the global ski gear and equipment industry was valued at around 1.26 billion US dollars in 2020. It is forecast to grow to 1.6 billion US dollars by 2025.

Ski by the Numbers

In 2021, Germany operated the highest number of ski resorts – 498! But who rounded out the Top 10?

2. Russia – 354

3. Italy – 349

4. France – 317

5. Austria – 253

6. Sweden – 228

7. Norway – 213

8. Czech Republic – 191

9. Switzerland – 183

10. Poland – 182

CHAPTER
THREE

Run, Skier, Run

With our skis dangling perilously over the edge of the peak of the plunge, it's time to push your poles into the powder and pray to Ullr and Skade for a wild ride down. Open your eyes, breathe in the majesty of the mountain – there's no place better to feel alive. See you at the bottom. The slowest down buys the first shot…them's the rules.

According to the 2020 International Report on Snow & Mountain Tourism, there are 80 nations that operate ski tourism at dedicated ski areas. An additional 20 countries have mountainous places to ski, but no lifts or resorts.

St Bernard

The patron saint of skiers is
the eleventh-century monk,
St Bernard of Menthon.

Bernard was proclaimed patron and
protector of skiers following his 40
years of missionary work throughout
the Alps. He built schools and
churches, as well as two mountain
hospices to help travellers lost between
passes. Pope Pius XI canonized
Bernard in 1923. Following the
sainthood, alpine herding and rescue
dogs were renamed (from Barry Dogs)
in his honour: the St Bernard.

Rules of the Road

Skiing may look like disorganized chaos, but there are mountain rules to obey:

1. Respect all other skiers, no matter their ability.

2. Know your ability; and always control your speed and balance.

3. Those who are below you on the slope always have the right of way.

4. Leave plenty of space when you are overtaking another skier. No tailgating and bumrushing!

5. Always look up the slope before merging onto a new piste.

6. Don't stop on a slope unless absolutely necessary. If you must, stop at the side.

7. If you fall over, make your way to the side of the slope, if possible.

8. Respect all mountain signs and markings.

9. If you witness an accident, stop to help. Then call ski patrol.

10. If you collide with another skier, you must swap ID for insurance purposes.

Steeze

When "style" and "ease" come together, they describe a skier's effortless elegance.

Are you a steezy skier?

Sendy

A route or line on a slope that offers ample opportunity for gnarly skiing.

"That line's looking sendy!"

Switch

Riding backwards on your skis? You're doing a bitchin' switchin'.

What do skiers get
from sitting on the
snow too long?

Polaroids.

The most popular alcoholic après-ski drink is known by many names, depending on where you are.

Mulled wine, vin chaud, vin brulé, glühwein – it's all the same: warm red wine infused with spices such as cinnamon and orange, and a sprinkle of sugar.

Après-Ski Drinks #4: Switzerland

According to sno.co.uk, these are the top après-ski drinks in Switzerland:

Jägerbomb: Jägermeister shot dropped into a half pint of Red Bull. Chug in one.

Hypokras: Warm white wine, red wine, black tea, cinnamon, sugar, cloves, ginger, and oranges.

Glühmost: Warm apple cider with cinnamon, sugar, and fresh orange.

Schümli pflümli: Coffee and Zwetschgen schnapps, topped with whipped cream.

Kirsch: Cherry brandy made from sour morello cherry juice.

A Hot Toddy is perhaps the most popular après-ski tipple to topple Britons over on the slopes.

Tip a shot of whiskey (or rum, or brandy) into a mug, add boiled water, a spoonful of honey, a slice of lemon and a sprinkle of cinnamon. Heaven in a half shell.

66

It's better to go
skiing and think
of God than go
to church and
think of sport.

99

Fridtjof Nansen

66

There is
no such thing as
too much snow.

99

Doug Coombs

66

Everyone I know who skis is dead.

99

Will Ferrell

66

It is unbecoming for a cardinal to ski badly.

99

Pope John Paul II

You can't buy
happiness. But you
can buy a ski pass.

Skiing by Numbers: Most Popular Nations

According to the 2020 International Report on Snow & Mountain Tourism, these nations are the most popular skiing destinations, based on a five-year average of number of skiers.

United States – 51 million

France – 50 million

Austria – 50 million

Japan – 30 million

Italy – 28 million

Switzerland – 22 million

Canada – 18 million

China – 15 million

Sweden – 10 million

Germany – 10 million

Russia – 9 million

Norway – 9 million

Czech Republic – 8 million

Spain – 5 million

Poland – 5 million

Slovakia – 5 million

South Korea – 5 million

Finland – 3 million

Andorra – 3 million

Australia – 3 million

Jamie Stevenson (of the UK) has the world record for most countries skied in a single month – 17!

Countries skied in: Scotland, Spain, Andorra, France, Italy, Switzerland, Liechtenstein, Austria, Germany, Slovenia, Poland, Slovakia, Czech Republic, Estonia, Finland, Sweden, Norway.

Frozen

In 2013, Disney's Frozen became a worldwide phenomenon. You may have heard of it. However, in 2010, a "ski thriller" of the same name was released. Frozen tells the terrifying tale of three snowboarders stranded on a chairlift high up a mountain in Vermont. The boarders have one decision to make: stay on the chairlift and freeze to death, or jump. What would Elsa do?

According to the MET
Office, snowflakes take
about an hour to fall
to earth.

Eddie the Eagle

You know the name, now learn
the legend…

Michael David Edwards, or Eddie the
Eagle, is an English ski-jumper who, at
the Calgary Winter Olympics in 1988,
became the first competitor since 1928
to represent Great Britain in Olympic
ski jumping. At the Olympics, he
was ranked 55th in the world and
ultimately finished in last place in the
70m and 90m events. Today, Eddie the
Eagle is a synonym for underdog.

Not-So Snow White

Snow isn't white. It's translucent. When light strikes a snowflake, it bends and is scattered across the visible light spectrum as white light by the imperfections within the ice crystal. The same goes for anything with a crystalline structure – sugar, or salt, for example.

The oldest confirmed evidence of a set of wooden skis and sled runners were found near Lake Sindor in Russia, and date to around 6300 BC.

Luxury Ski

Skiing is a sport most enjoyed by the rich and famous. If you want to keep up with them, hang out at the world's most luxurious and exclusive ski resorts, as awarded by Ski Solutions:

1. Gstaad, Switzerland

2. Cortina, Italy

3. Zermatt, Switzerland

4. Aspen, USA

5. Courchevel, France

6. Lech, Austria

7. St Moritz, Switzerland

8. Megève, France

9. Vail, USA

10. Whistler, Canada

"

The first fall of snow is not only an event, it is a magical event. You go to bed in one kind of a world and wake up in another quite different.

"

J.B. Priestley

> **"**
>
> # To appreciate the beauty of a snowflake, it is necessary to stand out in the cold.
>
> **"**

Aristotle

During the 2020–2021 ski season, the US ski industry shrunk by $2 billion due to the coronavirus pandemic.

Jib

Skiing across anything that isn't snow.

For example, a rail, or a log.

Skiers who go jibbing are called jibbers.

"

Cross-country skiing is great if you live in a small country.

"

Steven Wright

When Hell freezes over… I'll ski there too.

The now-legendary Bond ski jump from *The Spy Who Loved Me* (1977) was inspired by a photo the film's producer, Michael G. Wilson, saw for an advert of Canadian Club Whisky, where a skier is seen jumping out of a helicopter.

The tagline read, "If you Space Ski Mount Asgard...before you hit the ground, hit the silk!". The stuntman used in the ad, Rick Sylvester, was hired for all Bond's earliest ski stunts.

On March 26, 2016, in Vars, France, Ivan Origone (of Italy) broke the world record for fastest men's skier when he reached 158.4 mph (254.9 km/h)!

The same day, Valentina Greggio (of Italy), became the world's fastest female on skis, reaching a speed of 153.5 mph (247 km/h).

What a day!

The US's first ski resort, Howelsen Hill in Steamboat Springs, Colorado, opened its slopes in 1915. The area has also produced more than 100 US Winter Olympians.

In 1721, Norway became the first country to operate a specialized ski unit in their army.

Today, every nation with a military has a specialized ski division.

It was Canadian skier,
Alex Foster who, in 1931, built
the first working rope tow – a
rope that skiers simply hold on
to with their hands to propel
them up the mountain.

Within three years, the
device was employed at other
Canadian slopes.

Danger Runs

The world's most challenging and dangerous ski runs, according to *National Geographic*, are:

Corbet's Couloir, Jackson Hole, Wyoming, USA

La Pas De Chavanette, Portes Du Soleil, France/Switzerland

Delirium Dive, Banff, Alberta, Canada

Grand Couloir, Courchevel, France

The Fingers, Squaw Valley, California, USA

Tortin, Verbier, Switzerland

Paradise, Mad River Glen, Vermont, USA

The Streif, Kitzbühel, Austria

Christmas Chute, Alyeska, Alaska, USA

Harakiri, Mayrhofen, Austria

One in a Million

According to the National Ski Areas Association, there is one ski-related fatality for every million skiers globally each year.

During the 2018/2019 ski season, there were 42 reported deaths. The main cause of these fatalities were collisions with other skiers, or other obstacles.

Australia is not just dry bush
and desert outback.

It has five major downhill ski resorts:
Perisher and Thredbo in New South
Wales, and Mount Buller, Falls Creek
and Mount Hotham in Victoria.

Due to the large surface area
– 1.6 million hectares! – and relative
proximity to the ocean, more snow
falls annually in Australia than all
of Switzerland. (Though it never
gets too deep.)

låt oss åka skidor!

"Let's go skiing!"
in Swedish.

CHAPTER
FOUR

Avant et *Après*

The best thing about skiing is that even when it ends for the day, there's still a lot more après-skiing to do. What other sport can you say that about? Today, après-skiing is big business for resorts, and its legend is rooted in one beautiful purpose: to unite skiers over their love of skiing…and partying! See you at the T-bar…

Après Ski Drinks #5: Canada

According to sno.co.uk, these are the top après-ski drinks in Canada:

Caesar: Bloody Mary – vodka, tabasco sauce, Worcestershire sauce and tomato juice.

Canadian whisky: Crown Royal will do.

Vidal blanc: Canadian dry white wine.

At the end of a long day's skiing, the sport's inventors in Norway would traditionally enjoy Aquavit as their après-ski tipple of choice.

Aquavit is made just like gin, but with caraway seeds instead of juniper berries.

"

Snow skiing is not fun. It is life, fully lived, life lived in a blaze of reality.

"

Dolores LaChapelle

Sometimes it's all about the win, sometimes it's all about the skiing.

Bode Miller

66

If you want to get a good taste of powder, first you have to eat some.

99

Bob Barnes

66

Just ski down there and jump off something for crying out loud.

99

Shane McConkey

"

I'm an après-ski girl.

"

Mariah Carey

66

I now realize that the small hills you see on ski slopes are formed around the bodies of forty-seven-year-olds who tried to learn snowboarding.

99

Dave Barry

Life is best when it's going downhill.

" You are one with your skis and nature. This is something that develops not only the body but the soul as well, and it has a deeper meaning for people than most of us perceive. "

Fridtjof Nansen

Mashed Potatoes
A skier's term for wet,
lumpy, heavy snow.

Bunny Slope

Otherwise known as a nursery slope; it's the lowest part of the mountain with a gradual decline, ideal for beginner skiers.

World's Most Popular Ski Resorts

According to the 2020 International Report on Snow & Mountain Tourism, these are the Top 12 ski resorts in the world.

1. Ski Arlberg, Austria

2. La Plagne, France

3. Campiglio Dolomiti di Brenta, Italy

4. SkiWelt Wilder Kaiser Brixental, Austria

5. Les Arcs, France

6. Whistler Blackcomb, Canada

7. Saalbach Hinterglemm Leogang Fieberbrun, Austria

8. Ischgl Silveretta Arena, Switzerland

9. Val Gardena, Italy

10. Val Thorens / Orelle, France

11. Flachau-Wagrain-St Johann, Austria

12. Breckenridge, Colorado, USA

In 1962, US skier Bob Lange
invented the first plastic
ski boots. They still had laces.

The hinged cuff was invented
in 1965 – by Lange.

By 1970, Lange's boots had been
universally accepted. Today,
they remain the boot to beat.

The very first commercial ski film was released a century ago, on December 23, 1920. *Das Wunder des Schneeschuhs* (*The Wonder of Snowshoes*), Arnold Fanck's documentary, follows an expedition 4,000 metres up the Swiss Alps. The cameras capture footage of downhill skiers showing off the pioneering Arlberg Technique, created by Hannes Schneider, as well as other tricks, stunts, jumps and leaps.

They even film an avalanche.

The world's first chairlift –
literally two single chairs
propelled by a drive terminal
up Sun Valley Resort, Omaha,
was first turned on in 1936.

It was invented by Union
Pacific Railway engineer,
James Curran.

Thredbo, New South Wales,
is home to Australasia's
longest ski run – the Thredbo
Supertrail. Nearly 6 kilometres
(3.7 miles) of pure thigh-
burning bliss! How quickly
could you make it down?

These days, world-class speed skiers can reach more than 150mph. However, most intermediate skiers on resort slopes reach, on average, 20mph. Expert downhill racers can achieve 40–60mph.

Highest Ski Resorts in the World

1. Jade Dragon Snow Mountain, 4,700m (China)

2. Gulmarg, 3,980m (India)

3. Breckenridge, 3,914m (USA)

4. Zermatt, 3,899m (Switzerland)

5. Loveland, 3,871m (USA)

6. Tochal, 3,850m (Iran)

7. Chamonix, 3,842m (France)

8. Mt. Elbrus, 3,840m (Russia)

9. Telluride, 3,831m (USA)

10. Aspen Snowmass, 3,813m (USA)

Mogul Moguls

Mogul skiing is a highly competitive event at the Winter Olympics, and in World Skiing Championships. Commonly, competitors race down a 26-28 degree slope that's between 200 and 270 metres long, with moguls spaced around 3.5 metres apart. At the top and bottom of the course, competitors must perform acrobatic jumps.

60 per cent of the judges' scoring is based on mogul turn technique; 20 per cent on speed; and 20 per cent on the quality of the jumps.

Swiss ski mountaineer and mechanical engineer, Ernst Constam, invented the world's first J-bar in 1934, and the T-bar, in 1935. Both inventions caught on and were soon elevating skiers to new heights in Europe and the US.

According to the National Ski Areas Association, you can go alpine skiing in 37 of the 50 US states.

Aomori City, in the Tōhoku region of northern Japan, is the snowiest place on the planet. It receives approximately 312 inches of snowfall per year, due in part to its proximity to the Sea of Japan.

Andiamo a sciare!

"Let's go skiing!"
in Italian.

Chionophobia
is an intense fear
of snow.

Top 10: Most popular ski resorts in the US in 2022

1. Vail Ski Resort, Colorado

2. Aspen/Snowmass, Colorado

3. Snowbird, Utah

4. Park City Mountain Resort, Utah

5. Telluride Ski Resort, Colorado

6. Jackson Hole Mountain Resort, Wyoming

7. Breckenridge Ski Resort, Colorado

8. Beaver Creek, Colorado

9. Deer Valley, Utah

10. Steamboat, Colorado

Ski Runs by Colour

Green – Beginner

Blue – Intermediate

Red – Advanced

Black – Expert

Black single/double diamond – Expert

Black triple diamond – Extreme

Skiing Playlist #2: Accessories

"Poles Apart" – Pink Floyd

"Goggles" – Melvins

"Ice Ice Baby" – Vanilla Ice

"Ain't No Mountain High Enough"
– Marvin Gaye

"Powder On My Clothes" – Snoop Dogg

"Keep Your Powder Dry" – Motörhead

"Rocky Mountain High" – John Denver

"High On A Mountain Top"
– Loretta Lynn

"Whose Bed Have Your Boots Been In"
– Shania Twain

"Get On Your Boots" – U2

There's no actual time that après-ski officially begins, though most skiers agree that 4 p.m. feels right.

The first feature film to showcase lots of skiing was 1936's crime drama *Hideout in the Alps*, or *Dusty Ermine* as it was known in the UK.

Brits Abroad

More than 1.7 million Brits* go skiing every year. If you want to avoid them, don't go to these resorts, as they are where they go the most…

1. Tignes, France

2. Val d'Isère, France

3. St Anton, Austria

4. Les Arcs, France

5. La Plagne, France

6. Meribel, France

7. Val Thorens, France

8. Alpe d'Huez, France

9. Les Deux Alpes, France

10. Courchevel, France

The first plastic fiberglass ski was invented by Fred Langendorf and Art Molnar in 1959.

By 1968, recreational sport skies were no longer made of wood or aluminium.

Shin-bang

You know this feeling well.
Shin-bang is the discomfort
you feel in the lower anterior
portion of the shin (tibia)
caused by prolonged pressing of
the shin against the tongue of
a ski boot. An après-ski or two
will help the pain float away.

During the 2019/20 season, a total of 470 ski resorts were operational in the US.

Since 1990, 30 ski resorts have closed for business.

Lass uns Ski fahren gehen!

"Let's go skiing!"
in German.

In 2022, according to the 2021 International Report on Snow & Mountain Tourism, there are 13 million annual skiers in mainland China – just 1 per cent of the population.

66

Life is like skiing. Just
like skiing, the goal is
not to get to the bottom
of the hill. It's to have
a bunch of good runs
before the sun sets.

99

Seth Godin

66

Some of the events in the Olympics
don't make sense to me. I don't
understand the connection to any
reality... Like in the Winter Olympics
they have that biathlon that combines
cross-country skiing with shooting
a gun. How many alpine snipers
are into this? Ski, shoot a gun... ski,
bang, bang, bang... It's like combining
swimming and strangling a guy.

99

Jerry Seinfeld

66

Only men who
have worn a ski suit
understand how
complicated it is for
a woman to go to the
bathroom when she's
wearing a jumpsuit.

99

Rita Rudner

66

Feel the mountain
and let it show you how
you're going to ski it.
Relax and cruise. This
isn't a fight, it's a dance,
and the mountain
always leads.

99

Jim Bowden

Milk Run

A skier's first run of the day. Blows away hangovers.

66

There is nothing in the world like going out onto an untouched, open, virgin mountain slope, drenched under a thick blanket of new powder snow. It gives a supreme feeling of freedom, mobility. A great sense of flying, moving anywhere in a great white paradise.

99

Hans Gmoser

CHAPTER
FIVE

Lift-off!

Skiers live for amplitude: that feeling of taking off and getting high on Mother Nature's white powder. They are thrill-seekers, adrenaline junkies, daredevils, swish-bucklers, earthly epicureans, ski sybarites – and they'll do anything for their next hit of fresh snow. Let's see what shenanigans they get up to on the next run…

Wipe Out

Falling head over
heels in love with
the taste of snow in
spectacular fashion.

66

The sport of skiing consists of
wearing three thousand dollars'
worth of clothes and equipment
and driving two hundred miles
in the snow in order to stand
around at a bar and get drunk.

99

P.J. O'Rourke

Six Sides of the Snowflake

When frozen water molecules attach themselves to a pollen or dust particle in the sky, they create an ice crystal, or snowflake.

Water molecules are shaped like a V – it has two hydrogen atoms and one oxygen atom – so when they align and freeze together, they form a hexagonal shape. As the snowflake falls, more water molecules bond to it, but are only evenly added to the hexagon, so the shape never changes.

As it descends, the snowflake increases in size while maintaining its six sides!

The origin of the French word "salopettes" is *saloper*, meaning "to make dirty".

In 1937, the sticky solution to inventing a better ski became unstuck when R.E.D. Clark, in Cambridge, invented Aerolite, a formaldehyde-based adhesive, that was specifically designed to glue aeroplanes together.

On skis, it allowed metal and plastic to be stuck together forever.

4,500 years ago, a carving of a skier was imprinted on stone in Rodoy, Norway.

The age of the carving was established using carbon dating. It is the first written evidence of skiing.

If you have a fear of steep slopes, don't worry, you're just bathmophobic.

Skiing is great for the mind, but even better for your body. A decent ski stance naturally keeps your body in a squat position, which helps strengthens your core, quads, hamstrings, calves and glutes.

World's Weirdest Skiing

According to *World Travel Guide*, these are the 19 weirdest places to go skiing in the world:

1. Masikryong, North Korea

2. Mauna Kea, Hawaii

3. Bamyan, Afghanistan

4. Malam Jabba, Pakistan

5. Dizin, Iran

6. Chréa, Algeria

7. Tiffindell, South Africa

8. Mt Hermon, Israel

9. Oukaïmeden, Morocco

10. Mt Etna, Sicily

11. Afrikiski, Lesotho

12. Ben Lomond, Tasmania, Australia

13. Mzaar Kfardebian, Lebanon

14. Mt Olympus, Cyprus

15. Gulmarg, India

16. Jahorina, Bosnia and Herzegovina

17. Fan Mountains, Tajikistan

18. Cerro Castor, Argentina

19. Union Glacier Camp, Antartica

Orophobia is the fear of mountains.

66

A person should have
wings to carry them
where their dreams go,
but sometimes a pair
of skis makes a good
substitute.

99

Hans Gmoser

"

All things are possible … except skiing through a revolving door.

"

Woody Allen

Skiing is the only sport
where you spend an
arm and a leg to break
an arm and a leg!

Ecole du Ski Français

The world's largest ski school is Ecole du Ski Français, in France. The organization has more than 250 schools throughout the Alps and employs 15,000 ski instructors each season.

The instructors can be easily spotted on the slopes with their famous red jackets.

The first recorded
downhill skiing race
was held in Sweden
in 1879. It was also the
same year the word
"slalom" first appeared.

Alpine, or downhill, skiing debuted and the 1936 Winter Olympics. German-born Franz Pfnür won the first gold medal for the event.

Blue Bird

A term a skier would use to describe a beautiful sunny day with clear blue skies.

The most inexpensive adult day lift pass in Europe in 2022 was in Bosnia & Heregovina's Bjelasnica ski region.

Ski's the Limit

According to Crystalski, these are the best-value lift passes in Europe in the local Euros:

1. Dolomites (Italy) – 23 cents per km.

2. Zillertal (Austria) – 39 cents per km.

3. Portes du Soleil (France/Switzerland) – 39 cents per km.

4. The Three Valleys (France) – 49 cents per km.

5. The Milky Way (Italy/France) – 52 cents per km.

*La Clusaz and Chamrousse (France) is free.

La oss gå på ski

"Let's go skiing!"
in Norweigan.

It's better to be safe than cool: wearing a helmet while skiing can reduce head injuries by up to 44 per cent.

According to Statista, 1.76 million Britons go on a ski holiday each year, a value of £3 billion to the skiing resort and equipment industry.

Skiers by Population

In 2021, residents of Liechtenstein held the honour of being the world's most ski-obsessed nation, by population size. 36 per cent of the population skies annually. Switzerland was second, with 35 per cent, and Austria third, with 34 per cent. In the UK, 10 per cent of the population goes skiing annually. Data from Statista.

CHAPTER
SIX

Mountains and Moguls

Skiing is much more than just sliding down a slope in style. It's about technique, trigonometry, becoming one with the mountain, and learning how to read the myriad conditions that could affect your run and adapting your approach to each slope. Remember: the better you ski, the harder you fall. Welcome to ski school…

66

Skiing is the next best thing to having wings.

99

Oprah Winfrey

Gaper

A skier who annoys other skiers by not observing a resort's code of conduct.

Never-ever

A virgin skier.*

*Not a skier who's also a virgin.

Pizza

A popular alternative
term to describe a
snowplough.

French Fries

The opposite of pizza; a popular alternative term to describe the skis moving in parallel while skiing downhill and parallel turning.

Skijoring

A skier being pulled over snow by a means of transport, such as a horse or vehicle.

Bomber

An out-of-control skier.

First Tracks

The first morning tracks on a run for all other skiers to see. A badge of honour.

Also known as Freshies.

Pow

Fresh powder
snow. Bliss.

Skiing is the most popular winter snow sport in the US.

In 2022, according to Statista, there were 14.94 million annual skiers in the US, twice as many as the 7.56 million snowboarders.

The Alps receive 43 per cent of all skier days globally, approximately 210 million skiers a season. Norden nations – Sweden, Norway and Finland – receive roughly 20 million skiers a season.

As of 2022, there are roughly 2,000 alpine skiing destinations in the world.

According to Statista, only 13 per cent of French people ski.*

*Remarkable, considering the French have the best skiing in the world!

The world's first recorded ski jumper was Danish war hero, Olaf Rye. In November 1808, he got air – 9.5 metres (3 feet) of it! – in front of an audience of soldiers near the Eidsberg Church, in Viken County.

The Zermatt Matterhorn Ski Resort, Switzerland, is the only ski destination in the world that offers an "absolute snow guarantee" – it promises 365 days of snowfall.